TRAINS
OF THE ISLE of MAN

Post nationalisation

STAN BASNETT

Published on the Isle of Man by
Lily Publications, PO Box 33, Ramsey, Isle of Man IM99 4LP
Tel: +44 (0)1624 898446   Fax: +44 (0)1624 898449
E-mail: info@lilypublications.co.uk   Web: www.lilypublications.co.uk

POST NATIONALISATION

This is the third book in the Transport Features of the Isle of Man series on trains of the Isle of Man and covers the period between 1978 and 2008.

1978 was the year that the Isle of Man Government finally acquired the trackbed and adjoining land of the disused railway lines between Douglas, Peel and Ramsey including St. John's to Foxdale. Included in the purchase was the whole of the railway from Douglas to Port Erin together with all the locomotives and rolling stock.

The company which had been struggling to run the railway for the last decade or more, to satisfy its statutory duty to operate, was in a poor state. Restrained by the provisions contained in the Railway Acts and at the same time the demands of its shareholders who saw the value of their stock diminishing, the company had no alternative other than to realise its assets. By the time the Government stepped in only the Port Erin line was left and some historic rolling stock had gone, either scrapped or sold privately. It was a close call.

With responsibility for the operation of the steam railway placed under the control of the Manx Electric Railway Board, their first task was to assess what required to be done. The track was in need of urgent maintenance, something that continually appeared in the Railway Inspector's reports. This was due entirely to the fact that the company had not spent sufficient money on maintenance. The locomotives and rolling stock were run down and all in desperate need of overhaul. Only five locomotives were considered serviceable at the time of takeover and they were: *No.4 Loch*, *No.10 G.H.Wood*, *No.11 Maitland*, *No.12 Hutchinson* and *No.13 Kissack*. The fact that so many were usable was as a result of the financial investment by Lord Ailsa during the time that he had run the railway.

With an influx of new politicians and an enthusiastic staff from the Manx Electric Railway the future looked promising. The staff at the Manx

Locomotive **No.4 Loch** was the first to be operated by the Manx Electric Railway Board on nationalisation.

Electric were well used to railway enthusiasts and much more aware of the heritage value of the Island's railway systems than the old company ever were. There was, however, a long way to go.

Progressive track renewal was soon to become a regular feature on the railway every winter. Much needed repairs to locomotives and rolling stock were commenced and a new boiler was ordered for *No.12 Hutchinson*. The first obvious sign that serious investment in the railway was forthcoming happened at the end of the first season. Contractors moved in on Nunnery Bridge across the Douglas River and commenced work on its removal. During the winter a new bridge was erected and tested to the satisfaction of the Railway Inspector in March 1979.

With numerous anniversaries coming up every opportunity was taken by the new regime to celebrate them with special events. The railway press enthused and the new order had stamped its mark. My good friend Peter Craine, so long an enthusiast of the railway was successfully elected to the House of Keys, the Island's Parliament, and became Chairman of the Manx Electric Railway Board. Yet another reassuring sign for the future of the steam railway.

No.14 Thornhill was sold locally and still remains in local ownership. *No.8 Fenella* was also sold privately. Both purchasers were known sympathisers to the railway cause and, presumably mindful of what had gone before were prepared to ensure that at least two of the locomotives would survive into the future. In the event *No.8* was to eventually to return to service on the railway under an agreement between the owner and the IOM Government as the operator.

No.3 Pender was sold to the Museum of Science and Industry in Manchester where it remains as a

cut away exhibit showing the workings of a steam locomotive, a fitting tribute to the Gorton Foundry and Beyer Peacock.

No.12 Hutchinson meanwhile was the first to receive a new boiler and emerged from the shops sporting a new square cab and controversially painted blue. With a view to forthcoming celebrations of various anniversaries *No.15 Caledonia* and *No.1 Sutherland* were removed from the Museum at Port Erin and taken to Douglas for complete overhauls. This was in addition to the work in progress on *No.10 G.H.Wood* which was already undergoing a major overhaul.

The first Enthusiasts Weeks were relatively low key by comparison with what was to come but *No.4 Loch* was the first locomotive to run on Manx Electric rails to the Dhoon. Without doubt the ultimate event took place in 1995 to celebrate the

The sad condition of the locomotive workshop in 1978 was a clear indication that not everything that had been removed in 1975 had found its way back into Douglas. The building itself was showing signs of the years of neglect to the condition of the roof with damp and mildew growing on the walls.

Perhaps the biggest problem that the Manx Electric Railway Board (later National Transport) inherited when they took over responsibility for the railway was the condition of the track. Derailments were commonplace, particularly with *No.13 Kissack* running bunker first, even as late as 1983 when the hapless locomotive came off the rails within the confines of Douglas Station and once again running bunker first.

Centenary of the Snaefell Mountain Railway when the reason for the refurbishment of *No.15 Caledonia* became apparent. The fact that the original contractor who built the line had used the locomotive was enough to bring it out of retirement for the event. A temporary third rail to the correct gauge was laid between Bungalow Halt and Summit Station to allow the locomotive to run and the rest as they say is history.

Steam on Snaefell with the locomotive running between the Bungalow and the summit presented an unforgettable experience, particularly as it was pushing a tram trailer in which people could, for a fee, ride to the top propelled by a steam locomotive. It brought enthusiasts from all over the world to the Island. The locomotive then entered general service and still remains in service with the troublesome injector problems solved at long last. It must be said that it has been hard to keep up with the various liveries it has since carried. The colour in which it emerged for the Centenary celebrations matched its original Manx Northern Railway livery perfectly, a sample of its original paint having being found on the valve gear eccentrics.

Various events between 1992 and 1997 saw *No.4 Loch*, *No.15 Caledonia* and *No.1 Sutherland* running on the Manx Electric Railway, the latter between Laxey and South Cape and the others between Laxey and the Dhoon. Although the purists may have had mixed feelings about steam railway on the electric tramway the up side of it all was that the steam railway did get additional locomotives into service. It was an extraordinary time in the history of the steam railway which certainly provided many exciting opportunities for unusual photographs.

Stations at Castletown and Port Erin have been refurbished and new carriage sheds built at Douglas and Port Erin. With much of the track now replaced and Douglas Station reduced in size to accommodate the new central bus garage for National Transport's bus fleet, the railway was well placed for the 21st century.

It has been difficult for me to strike a balance with the photographs to show what has happened during this interesting period of the railway's history. I have deliberately selected some of the more unusual aspects to give an insight into the workings of the railway and sincerely hope that you the reader enjoy them. I have noticed whilst selecting the photographs many familiar faces recording the events and realised that I must appear on their photographs just as they on mine!

In conclusion I would like to say a big thank you to all of the staff of the railway past and present who have tolerated my presence and my camera over the last fifty years.

The railway would appear now to be going through yet another metamorphosis as the Heritage Railway but that will be another story for someone else to tell.

No.14 Thornhill being placed on a low-loader for transport to its new home on the Island.

Preparing for the 1978 season the railcars and the Whickham tram were seen in use with the permanent way gang on track maintenance at Ellenbrook Farm where problems with a culvert were notorious.

No.13 Kissack, here crossing the embankment over the Santon Burn on the approach to Santon Station, was the other mainstay of the first season of operation under nationalisation.

Time had stood still for many years for the time clock which was still in its place gathering dust at the time of the takeover. I don't know where it went but when you saw the number of dockets it is indicative of the importance of the railway by the number of persons employed within the engineering section.

Under Government ownership a new Railway Inspector was appointed and he made several inspections of the Nunnery Bridge, the outcome of which was that it was condemned. Work started on its demolition in October 1978 after the last train of the season had run.

The new bridge had been prefabricated by Wilson & Collins, a local firm of steel fabricators, and assembly was completed without problem. The first test run with *No.13 Kissack* took place before the start of the 1979 season.

My friend and fellow enthusiast Peter Craine was now a member of the House of Keys, the Island's Parliament. He was appointed to the position of Chairman of the Manx Electric Railway Board and as such was responsible now for the steam railway. It was not surprising to see him very much "hands on" on this occasion. In fact we both now had official responsibilities which involved the railway.

No.4 Loch climbing out of Keristal Cutting and nearing the Keristal summit. *No.4* and *No.13* were the two locomotives in the best condition following the investment by Lord Ailsa and not surprisingly carried the bulk of the traffic initially on nationalisation.

The boiler of **No.12 Hutchinson** had failed its inspection in 1978 and the railway had no option other than to order a replacement. As with all major overhauls the opportunity was taken to strip the locomotive down completely. Here work is well advanced with pistons and valves out of the cylinders and valve chests.

The new boiler for **No.12** soon after its arrival in 1979 from the UK boilermakers Israel Newton and ready for lifting into the chassis, once work on the steam chest and the running gear had been completed.

Through 1979 and 1980 locomotive availability was problematic. The railway hadn't recovered from the years of neglected maintenance by the Isle of Man Railway Company and was only surviving by the investment put in by Lord Ailsa. The result of the first major investment by the Government was the emergence of **No. 12 Hutchinson** in 1981. The larger boiler and side tanks were the major differences but by far the most obvious were the "Mannin style" square cab and the controversial blue livery.

Early in 1982 a large mud slide occurred at Oakhill Cutting caused by a burst water main in the adjoining road which required the use of a mechanical digger to clear the obstruction. With the spoil being removed by **No. 12 Hutchinson** using what must have been the only serviceable trucks to have escaped the scrap man's torch.

No.4 Loch approaching the Blackboards bridge displaying the new maroon livery which was applied in 1978 before the start of that season.

No.11 Maitland at the Keristal summit, one of my favourite locations for photography, in 1980 at a time when it was suffering failures in traffic with boiler tubes blowing on a regular basis which eventually led to it receiving the boiler originally destined for **No.10 G.H.Wood.**

The first train of the day leaving Douglas for Port Erin having just cleared the Nunnery Cutting and crossing the Nunnery cattle creep, showing the height of the embankment here. The power station at Pulrose is commencing one of its many metamorphoses!

The railcars displayed several unusual colour schemes in the first years of nationnalisation none of which were really popular. One of the cars required major maintenance in 1979 which severely restricted their use and relegated the remaining serviceable one to fire-fighting duty.

The problem with derailment within the confines of the station still continued to be a problem emphasising the need for urgent track repair and highlighting the years of neglect with regard to track maintenance. The diesel railcars were used for station pilot duties due to the lack of available motive power in the early years of nationalisation and here the leading unit has split the points and derailed in big style.

I am aware that over the last few years there have been a number of publications which have well covered the modern scene. I said in the introduction that I would try and choose different photographs to cover some activities not normally seen. Here is **No.10 G.H.Wood** in the workshop preparatory to the driving wheels being drawn.

The lower photograph shows the chassis lifted clear to allow the wheels to drop out of the horn blocks and be wheeled clear.

I mentioned that **No.11 Maitland** had trouble during 1980 and 1981 with boiler tubes. At the end of the season it was decided after inspection that as this locomotive required very little work on the mechanical condition of its running gear the boiler destined for **No.10** would be fitted to **No.11**. This delayed the completion of **No.10 G.H.Wood** even further.

A photograph which twenty years earlier would have been impossible: the fireplace in the engineering workshop (the only means of heating) now back as if nothing had happened after the upset of 1975 (covered in the second book). It would eventually succumb to Health and Safety Regulations.

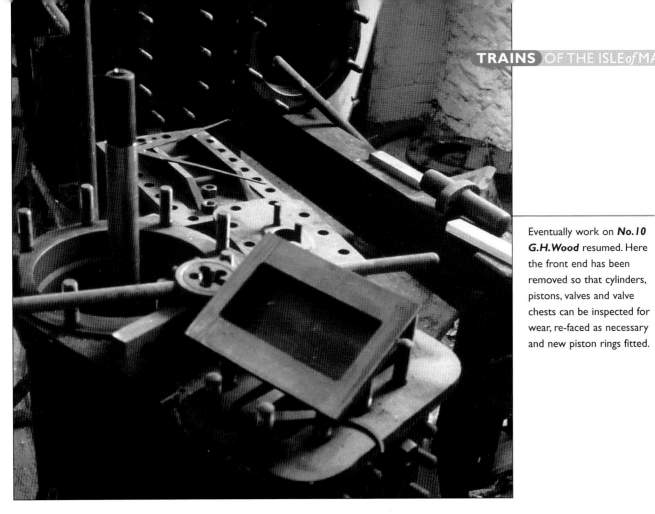

Eventually work on **No.10 G.H.Wood** resumed. Here the front end has been removed so that cylinders, pistons, valves and valve chests can be inspected for wear, re-faced as necessary and new piston rings fitted.

Still with **No.10** and Colin Goldsmith working on the wheel lathe, re-profiling the driving wheels using original wheel profile templates which had fortunately survived, thanks to Donald Shaw, through the last few years of the old company's existence when so much could have been lost.

No.10 was completely stripped down to the frames. The pony truck was removed and the wheels await their turn on the wheel lathe for re-profiling.

Here the chimney and brass dome cover, the latter in its protective covering of grease had been located from the stores and await final fitting. Considerable elbow grease, will be required from some poor unfortunate to bring the dome cover up to a fine polish aided by liberal amounts of paraffin and Brasso.

Colin Goldsmith working on one of the valve chests from *No.10*. Colin's premature death through illness robbed the steam railway of an enthusiastic stalwart with a huge amount of knowledge. He is sadly missed by many both within the railway and outside.

Here we see the front end of **No.10** with the cylinders and valve chests in place in the frames, new bolts and studs fitted and awaiting the pistons and valves before being closed up with the covers.

The valves essential to the proper functioning of a steam engine have been faced and are ready to be inserted into the valve chest.

Colin was a good personal friend but also a friend to many enthusiasts throughout the world as I found on a railway visit to Germany. Here he is adjusting the static valve timing on *No.10* with the motion now fitted as the rebuild progresses.

The new boiler for *No.10* now in the engineering workshops is receiving the insulating lagging prior to being lifted and dropped into the frames using the 10-ton travelling gantry crane.

The major overhaul of **No. 10 G.H. Wood** had started in the winter of 1977/78: however, mainly due to other priorities its completion was deferred on a number of occasions. It eventually emerged in 1993 in time to take part in the Year of the Railways activities. Colin Goldsmith here seen in a precarious position is working on the dome before fitting the cladding and finally the brass dome cover literally minutes before the locomotive made its inaugural public appearance.

Driver Jack Petrie prepares
No.10 G.H.Wood for the
day's work in Douglas
running shed.

Early in 1992 National Transport's Chief Executive Robert Smith together with Morris Faragher, Graham Warhurst and Colin Goldsmith visited a factory in East Germany. The purpose of the visit was to view a diesel locomotive of similar gauge to the IOM Railway that was being offered for sale. It was considered suitable after inspection and a deal was done.

The locomotive arrived by road and ferry direct from Germany on 18th July and was off-loaded from the step frame trailer and placed on Isle of Man Railway metals by local haulage and plant hire contractor Stephen Carter.

The following day a trial run was made to Port Soderick with seven coaches and this proved satisfactory. The next run to Port Erin revealed problems with the suspension which caused the locomotive to pitch at speed. The matter was resolved by fitting external hydraulic damping units, a trick learnt from experience with trams on the Manx Electric Railway. Considering that the locomotive was intended for shunting within a steel works it wasn't surprising.

In 1990 **No.12 Hutchinson** was withdrawn from service with a boiler defect which necessitated removal of the boiler from the chassis and its despatch to Ramsey Shipyard for attention. It didn't return until early in 1991.

The people of Port Erin were taken by surprise on a late September morning in 1993 with the sight of **No.15 Caledonia** passing through the village on a low-loader. It was being taken to Douglas to be made ready for celebrations in connection with the Centenary of the Snaefell Mountain Railway in 1995. *(Photo Gillian Basnett)*

Colin Goldsmith contemplates the problems ahead as the strip-down of **Caledonia** is commenced in the Douglas workshops. The locomotive revealed many of its secrets during the winter, the biggest being the condition of the boiler and the pannier tanks,

When the pannier tanks were removed it revealed severe wastage to the backs of the tanks which meant there was no alternative other than replacement. Preliminary inspection of the boiler also indicated wastage due to water having been left in the boiler when it was placed in the Museum. It would have to be sent to specialist boilermakers for repair.

With the tanks and boiler cladding removed Brian Cottier steam-cleans the boiler and smokebox. No, it is not in steam - that is steam from the steam lance coming out of the funnel! The dead loco was pulled out of the workshop by **No.17**, now being put to good use within Douglas Station.

During the strip-down *Caledonia* confirmed that its origins were from a much earlier age as it revealed a very early form of boiler lagging which used timber slats - almost certainly the original ones dating from 1885.

The wheels were removed from the frames and made ready to be placed in the wheel lathe. The boiler meanwhile now removed from the frames was set on the boiler dolly for removal outside, to be transferred to a road vehicle for shipment to the boilermakers Messrs H.A.McEwans near Keighley in West Yorkshire who were contracted to carry out the necessary repairs.

Since **Caledonia** had been repainted in a dark maroon during Lord Ailsa's stewardship and placed in the Railway Museum there had been much speculation about exactly what was the original colour of the locomotive in Manx Northern times. Because this was almost certainly the first occasion that the locomotive had been completely stripped down, some original paint had been found on the eccentrics and a tool box. Colin Goldsmith had a sample analysed, and the best match ever was determined and paint acquired for the repaint

Alex McBride, the man responsible for all the sign-writing and lining of the locomotives, applying the Hammerite paint to the wheels of **No.15** and for the first time we had a sample of what **Caledonia** would look like when restored to its new livery.

The wheels are in the frames and the boiler is being carefully lowered into position, the firebox being seated first.

The reassembly of *Caledonia* is nearly complete and the newly-fabricated steel pannier tanks of all-welded construction have been fitted. Alex McBride is fixing dummy rivet heads (affectionately known as chocolate drops) to replicate the originals prior to painting.

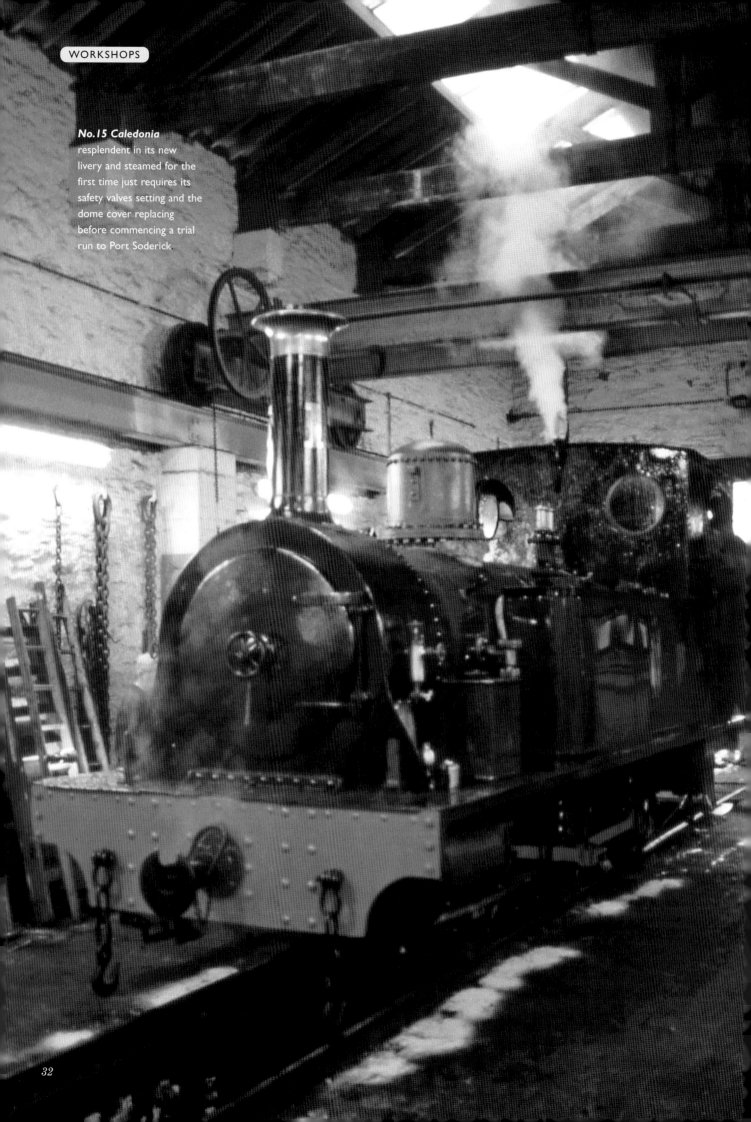

No.15 Caledonia resplendent in its new livery and steamed for the first time just requires its safety valves setting and the dome cover replacing before commencing a trial run to Port Soderick.

No.1 Sutherland was the next locomotive to be removed from Port Erin and taken to Douglas to be restored to full working condition. This time because of its location within the Museum it was pulled out on the track through the engine shed to be hauled to Douglas by **No.10 G.H.Wood**.

As before the main problem with these locomotives was that they had been cosmetically painted and placed in store in the Museum with very little attention to preservation. Now the major consideration was the condition of the boiler which was removed and also sent to Keighley for repair.

The wheels have been removed from **No.1** and already have been re-profiled and are ready to be put back in the horn blocks and offered up to the guides in the frames.

In order to get **Sutherland** back in service within the timescale needed a deal was done with the owners of **No.8 Fenella**, now in private ownership and being restored by the railway, that **No.8**'s boiler which was now back from the Severn Valley would be exchanged with **No.1**'s boiler when it returned from Keigthley.

Here the boiler is being inspected and hydraulically tested before being placed in **Sutherland's** frames

An interesting photograph in the late stages of assembly. The boiler end plate and the fire tubes can be seen before the blast pipe is fitted. A piston is clearly visible in one of the cylinders and as yet the valves need to be inserted. The front of the locomotive is supported on two re-railing jacks as the pony truck has not yet been fitted.

The rebuild of **No. 1 Sutherland** nears completion. The pony truck is on and Alex has performed his magic with the dummy rivets applied to the new welded side tanks.

John Elkin packs the lagging around the dome before fitting the brass dome cover as *No.1 Sutherland*, now complete and with steam being raised for final setting of the safety valves, sits outside the engineering workshop.

While all the work on restoring the steam locomotives to full working order fully occupied the railway staff, the diesel railcars, now in parlous condition, had been inspected for mechanical condition. It was decided to sub-contract the repair of the drive units to the Isle of Man Steam Packet's engineering section. The bodywork was known to be in need of repair but removal of some panelling found it to be worse than thought. A complete rebuild of the coachwork was started using joinery staff from other Government departments but in the railway shops. At present they remain unfinished and sit in the carriage shed at Douglas.

No.13 Kissack had returned to the Island in 2004 following its overhaul in the UK following National Transport's change in policy that all such work would be undertaken off Island. On its return to service problems were experienced with its wheels which involved their removal and return to the UK for remedial work to the defects to be undertaken.

In 1998 **No.4 Loch** was leased to the IOM Steam Railway Supporters Association for a period of 21 years and they had raised money towards a major overhaul which was undertaken at Chatham Steam Services in Kent during 2001. It returned to service late in 2002. During the 2004 season **Loch** had given trouble with its boiler and by February of 2005 it had been removed which revealed problems with the foundation ring. It was sent to the UK for repairs, being returned later in the year.

Here is the bottom half of **No.4 Loch** in February 2005 in the now covered area between the running shed and the carriage workshop after the boiler was removed.

Another view of work in progress in February 2005 on **No. 13 Kissack**, sitting on blocks waiting the return of its wheels. The boiler from **No.4 Loch** is sitting on the floor of the workshop on the right.

A lot has happened during the time the railway has been under Government ownership and the state of the track at the time of takeover was deplorable. A lot of work was undertaken by the permanent way gang in the early years and here are two examples. *No.4 Loch* is seen in the upper photograph moving runners loaded with rails out of Port Soderick to carry out much needed work at Santon. The lower photograph shows a work train with the railcars at the rear climbing past the White Hoe. This unusual combination was used to provide messing facilities for the workers engaged on the line. Now almost all of the line has been relaid by contractors laying transfer mains in connection with an all-island sewage processing plant at Santon, the remainder being carried out by the railway.

The decision to move the signal box may have been dictated by a planning condition attached to the permission for the new bus garage. Once the decision was made it gave the contractors and National Transport a major problem. The first task was to construct a raft under its footings and raise it to allow it to be moved intact.

The first attempts to move it by the contractor using tree-pulling equipment proved not to be successful as they could not overcome the initial friction. Stephen Carter, a local specialist contractor, was called in and employing appropriate vintage equipment was able to move the box to its new location.

The old carriage shed at Douglas in the process of being demolished and the ground cleared for the construction of the new bus garage and maintenance facility. The Douglas signal box has been moved to its new location.

The signal box now finally in its new location required underpinning and setting down on its new foundation.

The new trackwork between the platforms and the engineering workshops being inspected by Engineering Manager George Lawson and his assistant Darryl Gribbin.

The new carriage shed and its associated trackwork completed and in use on the former trackbed of the Peel line.

The engineering workshops and running sheds eventually received the long overdue expenditure on repairs to the roof, new electrical wiring and bringing into line with Health and Safety legislation as seen in this general view of the running shed with *No.15 Caledonia* resplendent in yet another new livery, an indulgence of David Howard, the newly-appointed Chief Executive.

The ventilation of the running shed was also improved and no longer was it the atmospheric place it used to be! Colin Goldsmith is admiring the recent acquisition of a Hunslet diesel locomotive which National Transport acquired from the contractor who reinstated the track after a main sewer was laid between Port Erin and the central disposal works at Santon along the railway trackbed.

I can probably quite truthfully say that not many people have been inside the clock tower on the ornamental gateway to the station steps at Douglas. There is not much room inside the tower but the original clock mechanism is intact and still operates the clock. This is the back of the clock face towards Athol Street. At the time of this visit the tower was showing signs of settlement no doubt as a direct result of the increased traffic on Peel Road (it was repaired in 1991). I do remember that Road Services double deck buses used to climb up Bank Hill into Peel Road which put them closer to the entrance than the present traffic. I also have a hang-up with public clocks in so far as I think they should always display the correct time. This clock seems to be stopped as I write this caption.

An unusual sight with **No.4 Loch** being used as a tree puller! There always have been problems with trees adjoining the track and the Island gets its fair share of gales with the result that trees, many in decline, are uprooted or lose limbs. This was the case on the approach to Nunnery Bridge and in the process of clearing **No.4** was used to extract the root of the offending tree.

Coach *No.F54* in the newly refurbished running shed is nearing completion and is ready for painting.

Here is the now fully restored workshop awaiting the installation of safety guards to the exposed belt drives from the overhead layshafts.

Robert Smith was the Chief Executive of National Transport during the time that many of the unusual events were held during the early 1990s. Without his enthusiasm and the support of David Cretney MHK, the Minister of the Department of Tourism and Leisure, as well as his leadership at grass roots level I suspect none of it might ever have happened. One of the first special steam events to be organised in connection with the 1993 Year of the Railways was a Travelling Post Office, part of a publicity stunt to launch the Isle of Man Post Office stamps celebrating the Centenary of the Manx Electric Railway.

Postman Jimmy Kelly travelled with the mail and used the bar area of the special train as his office to cancel the first day covers that travelled on the TPO Special.

Finally (below) here is the 'Special' at Ballasalla to collect mail posted in the temporary mail box situatied on the station platform. The event proved very popular and it turned out to be a very busy day for Jimmy.

A typical late summer scene as **No.11 Maitland** bursts through Ballabeg road bridge at speed with a good level run ahead to Colby. The fuchsia is in full bloom as is the hogweed! Many local people would prefer the fuchsia as the national flower rather than the cushag (ragwort) which is also a weed!

Now that **No.12 Hutchinson** is back to normal with a traditional wrap-over cab and in the Indian red livery we miss the beautiful shade of blue which many of us had slowly got to like! This photograph of the locomotive coasting down the Ballasalla bank past Ballabridson shows it to good effect. Driver Jack Petrie is looking out for the signal at Ballahick giving him the right of way to enter Ballasalla Station.

No.11 Maitland painted in a peculiar shade of green for the 1990 season crossing the delightful stone arched bridge over the Colby River on leaving Colby Station.

No.1 Sutherland in very unusual surroundings at Laxey Station prior to taking a steam special to South Cape as part of the Enthusiasts Week in 1998.

No.15 Caledonia also in unfamiliar territory as it climbs past Bulgham cliffs on its way to the Dhoon with one of the special trains to celebrate the International Railway Festival in 1995.

No.11 also back in its 'proper' Indian red livery runs alongside the Silverburn River as it coasts down into Castletown.

Jeffrey Kelly in charge of his regular engine *No.4 Loch* pauses at Santon Station with a Douglas-bound train in 1993 during the period that it was running chimney-first out of Port Erin.

No.4 Loch passing Ballastrang crossing at Santon with a rake of coaches in the purple lake livery which was not popular and also prone to fading, giving it a drab appearance.

A late afternoon photograph with *No.11 Maitland* stopped at Port Soderick to await the incoming train from Port Erin which passed at this station when operating the peak summer timetable.

No.11 Maitland starts to climb Ballasalla Bank as it passes Ballahick crossing showing the super elevation on the curve.

Nº 11

No.8 Fenella had been back in service since September 2003 and still remains in private ownership. It is now operated on the railway for which it was built and a true credit to all concerned in its preservation. Although I had a problem coming to terms with it sporting the sloping smokebox front - a minor price to pay for seeing it back in steam.

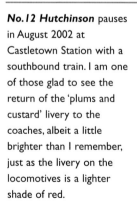

No.12 Hutchinson pauses in August 2002 at Castletown Station with a southbound train. I am one of those glad to see the return of the 'plums and custard' livery to the coaches, albeit a little brighter than I remember, just as the livery on the locomotives is a lighter shade of red.

No.4 Loch in its element and backing out of the running shed at Douglas to prepare for a day's work.

Here was the first indication of exciting things to come. We had seen the potential of the Enthusiasts Weeks but with significant anniversary dates imminent on the Manx Electric Railway it was clear that something was afoot. Stephen Carter took the chassis of **No.8 Fenella** to Laxey for clearance tests on the MER track north of Laxey.

Following the successful trials **No.4 Loch** was taken to Laxey and placed on the MER tracks for live steam trials as far as the Dhoon. Now the reason became clear: it was to commemorate the use of IMR **No.2 Derby** by the contractor building the line north of Laxey - seemed as good an excuse as any!

No.4 Loch was taken to Laxey at the end of November1991 behind Stephen Carter's trusty AEC. Matador tractor for live steam trials on the Manx Electric Railway track from Laxey to the Dhoon. Unloaded onto the tram tracks in Laxey Station the locomotive was taken to the tram sheds to be made ready for the first tests on Friday 29th November with two MER trailers in tow. The weather was dire and the track wet so it was a good test but badly let down by poor coal which had been a problem all season on the railway.

Before the press launch a number of runs were made to satisfy the Railway Inspector. **Loch** is approaching Bulgham on one of those runs, working hard in the winter conditions and on greasy rails. Winter may not have been the best time for the launch but it did provide the opportunity for some spectacular photographs!

No.4 Loch with trailers **No.57** and **No.58** leaves the car shed at Laxey to arrive at the station for the grand press pre-publicity launch of the Year of the Railways with two trams and a steam locomotive together in Laxey Station. It proved to be an excellent piece of public relations.

No. 4 Loch works hard as it approaches Skinscoe curve on the climb out of Laxey with the press launch special on Thursday 5th December 1991. The Engineering Superintendent Morris Faragher riding on the footplate. As a former Manx Electric man his knowledge of the track was to prove invaluable in the arrangement of these special events. They would never have been possible under the old regimes as it was definitely a 'never the twain shall meet' situation. It was one of the positive advantages resulting from nationalisation. These events and associated publicity put the Isle of Man and its railways firmly on the international map.

This view from above Bulgham shows *No.4 Loch* and *MER Tram No.1* with members of the press and running "wrong road" on the southbound track with the retinue of chasing cars. This would be repeated later in the day with members of the press in a double-deck bus following, full of press photographers taking more photographs.

We had already learnt that the reason **No.15 Caledonia** had been taken out of the Museum was in order to have it in steam for the Centenary of the Snaefell Mountain Railway. To squeeze the maximum publicity from the event it was decided to run it also from Laxey to the Dhoon following the success with **No.4 Loch**. While its boiler was away the chassis was taken to Laxey in March 1994 for clearance tests being propelled by **MER No.27**. Despite the locomotive being six-coupled it negotiated the sharp tramway curves without problem.

On completion of its major overhaul it was taken to the Bungalow on the Snaefell Mountain Railway and placed on temporary track for initial steam trials on 6th December 1994.

No.15 Caledonia at the Bungalow in March 1995 for final trials of additional fell braking required by the Railway Inspector. The weather on the first day of the trials was atrocious.

Two more photographs from the 1995 trials of **Caledonia** on Snaefell. The locomotive was moved forward from the newly-constructed siding onto the upward bound track to engage with the fell rail. Adjustments had to be carried out to the fell brake which involved fitters lying on their backs and working under the front of the buffer beam in snow flurries and a biting wind! Fortunately by the time runs were made for the Inspector's approval the weather had improved considerably.

Caledonia successfully made a number of runs on the Manx Electric Railway between Laxey and the Dhoon as part of the celebrations included in the 1995 International Railway Festival. In this photograph the locomotive has stopped on the viaduct at Laxey waiting clearance to run through the station to the special siding adjoining Ramsey Road from where the runs to the Dhoon commenced. The new injectors fitted during its major overhaul had cured the steaming problems completely.

Below: In addition during 1995 *No.15 Caledonia* ran a number of specials on the Isle of Man Railway metals, several of which were double-headed as in this photograph as it storms up the climb past the former White Hoe isolation hospital.

During Enthusiasts Week in 1998 the newly commissioned **No.1 Sutherland** was taken to Laxey to run special enthusiasts' trains between Laxey Station and South Cape. Here are two for the price of one: Two **No1s** in Laxey Station quite unique there aren't any others like them in the world with well over two hundred years between them!

No.1 simmers outside the tram shed at Laxey (in the time before the shed was partially demolished) as it is prepared for a day's work on the Manx Electric Railway. I never thought in my wildest dreams as a callow youth that anything like this would ever have been possible. These were halcyon days.

The special trips with Isle of Man Railway **No.1 Sutherland** to South Cape running "wrong road" and returning on the same track with **Manx Electric Railway No.1** running parallel proved enormously popular. They gave enthusiasts a rare opportunity to observe the motion of a steam locomotive working at close quarters. It was hard to say which was the more popular, riding behind a steam locomotive in an unusual setting or in a tram to photograph the action!

No.4 Loch a couple of years earlier making a vigorous ascent of what is known to the Manx Electric railway-men as 'Little Egypt' or more usually referred to as Dumbell's Bank. Both refer to its connection with the Laxey Mines and the spoil tips below this point. Another of those unbelievable events which no one ever foresaw.

The movement of steam locomotives between Douglas, Laxey and the Bungalow raised many eyebrows with the locals but for the enthusiasts it was a bonanza, none more so than when **No.4 Loch** was moved by not one but two Fowler BB1 road engines. Photographed at Groudle on 29th June 1993. The lead engine originally worked in road haulage for the firm of Norman E. Box and on this occasion was driven by the late Fred Dibnah.

Here **No.15 Caledonia** is being moved to Laxey by Stephen Carter and being hauled along Douglas promenade using a recently acquired Foden ballast tractor. The unit being found necessary for the movements up to the Bungalow the old Matador lacking the necessary grunt.

Another photograph of **No.4** on the MER this time crossing Minorca Bridge and photographed from the chasing tram. The photographer leaning out of one of the trailers is Robert Powell Hendry long time enthusiast and champion of the Isle of Man Railways. I can't imagine how many times he and I have appeared on each other's photographs over the years!

No.4 Loch back on familiar ground passes through Colby with a Steam 125 special in 1998, one of many run throughout the year.

All specials were not run in connection with enthusiasts' events. The three-car bar set proved immensely popular for group and corporate hire and in particular wedding parties. *No.12 Hutchinson* fully decorated with an appropriate headboard sits in Douglas Station on 31st May 1989 awaiting the arrival of a wedding party bound for Castletown..

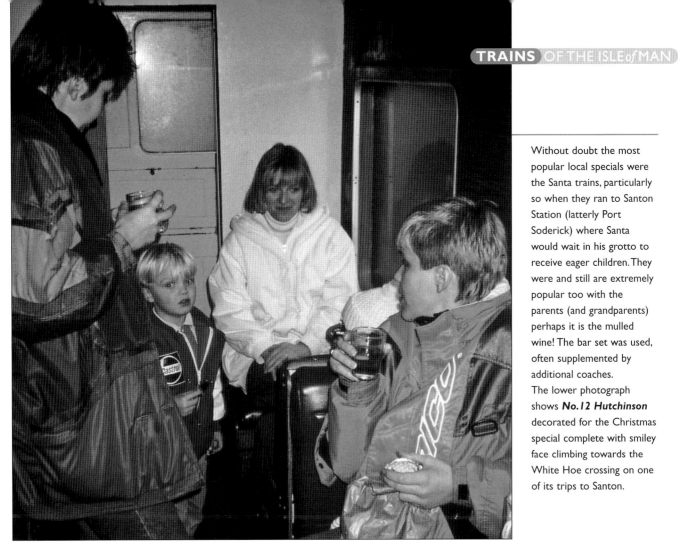

Without doubt the most popular local specials were the Santa trains, particularly so when they ran to Santon Station (latterly Port Soderick) where Santa would wait in his grotto to receive eager children. They were and still are extremely popular too with the parents (and grandparents) perhaps it is the mulled wine! The bar set was used, often supplemented by additional coaches.

The lower photograph shows *No.12 Hutchinson* decorated for the Christmas special complete with smiley face climbing towards the White Hoe crossing on one of its trips to Santon.

No.12 Hutchinson running round a Santa Special at Santon. The loco would then run past its train to take water at the water tank before coupling up for the run back to Douglas.

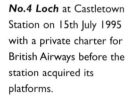

No.4 Loch at Castletown Station on 15th July 1995 with a private charter for British Airways before the station acquired its platforms.

A late afternoon shot of *No.11 Maitland* drifting through Crogga Glen with a Douglas bound train before the track was relaid.

Although special events and workshop photographs have taken up a large part of this book it is worth remembering that the greater part of the year was taken up with normal service trains maintaining the summer timetable. This section includes a selection of photographs of the railway going about its normal business.

In the upper photograph *No.11 Maitland* is climbing past the White Hoe crossing with a rake of coaches in the purple lake livery. In the lower photograph *No.4 Loch* is passing Lough Ned with a southbound train with driver Jeffrey Kelly in classic pose.

No.15 Caledonia double-heading with *No. 12 Hutchinson* crests Keristal Summit during 1995, the year of the International Railway Festival.

No.4 Loch on its regular duty and running the 'right way round' in the cutting approaching Santon Station with the coaches still in the purple lake livery applied during the early years of nationalisation.

I suspect that I was not alone with the difficulty in coming to terms with the different cab shape and the blue livery of **No.12 Hutchinson** when it re-entered service in 1981 as mentioned earlier. Here it is seen passing through the road bridge leaving Santon Station...

...its colour and cab shape did grow on us in time, it did prove extremely popular with the ladies and was in great demand for wedding specials. This photograph of **No.12** was taken at Keristal Summit which it crossed in spectacular style with a single-coach charter running before the service trains started. I have only witnessed one locomotive crossing the summit faster and that, believe it or not, was **Caledonia** on its first test run after its overhaul.

Two more photographs of *No.12 Hutchinson* in action. In the upper photograph it heads a train pulling into Castletown Station with driver Jack Petrie in charge. In the lower photograph it heads a train passing under the farm accommodation bridge at Ballakelly, Santon, fireman Brian Hays keeping a sharp look-out.

No.4 Loch has passed Ballastrang level crossing and is approaching the Blackboards overbridge. Compare the photograph on this page and page 54 with the photograph on page 93 in book two of this series to see how Ballastrang gatehouse has changed since it has been in private ownership as a private residence.

In a sylvan setting *No.11 Maitland*, now carrying brass numerals on its chimney, leaves Port Soderick on a gradual climb towards milepost 4 through one of the prettiest sections of the line.

A song may have been written about 'the last train to San Fernando' (yes I know it dates me) but here are a couple of 'lasts' on the IOM Railway. In the upper photograph the last train of the season emerges from Nunnery Cutting hauled by locomotive *No.11 Maitland* appropriately wearing a sad face. In the lower photograph *No.4 Loch* coasts into Port Soderick with the last train of the day from Port Erin.

Ballasalla level crossing has been through several metamorphoses. The top photograph shows it in its second re-incarnation within the period covered by the Transport Features series. The gates were capstan-operated from the cabin on the right using a series of chains within ducts in the roadway as originally installed (see book one in the series) but by the time this photograph was taken wear and tear was leading to problems, the gates didn't close properly and they were prone to failure. The third and current installation incorporates automatic drop barriers and new traffic signals replacing the earlier wig wag lights. These too have not been without their problems. The crossing still remains dangerous as its visibility is obscured to traffic approaching from the south.

No.15 Caledonia now with its injector problems well behind it and cylinder problems repaired after the end of its first season in service became a useful addition to the available motive power. It could be seen in regular service particularly at peak traffic times. It is seen at Douglas about to drop down onto a southbound train.

No.4 Loch working hard on a miserable day fights for grip approaching the White Hoe crossing.

The photographs in this section illustrate the south line as seen from the footplate. The first four photographs are taken from the footplate of **No.4 Loch**. This is the line as we leave Port Erin and approach Port St. Mary. In the right hand view, we approach the Castletown Bridge which carries Malew Road over the track. The driver and fireman have to keep a sharp look-out here for the Mill Road crossing and the signal for Castletown Station. Below, we are climbing out of Ballasalla on a gradient of 1 in 80 passing the disused Ballawoods gatehouse, now controlled by an automatic crossing.

This interesting driver's eye view is of Keristal rock cutting on the approach to Kewaigue road bridge.

There is no rest for the crew (below) on arrival at Douglas as the locomotive is released from the train and taken to the running shed for the fire to be cleaned, to fill with water and load coal by Selwyn Morgan, the fireman, before taking the next train back to Port Erin.

Now on the footplate of **No.10 G.H.Wood** in 1993. The engine is working hard as we climb the 1 in 65 gradient (above) through Nunnery Cutting and the climb continues at much the same gradient to the first summit of the line at Keristal.

Here (left) we are approaching the Blackboards bridge with the whistle warning of our approach. The Blackboards was so named because a screen of tarred boards was erected on both sides of the bridge soon after the line was built to stop smoke and steam from the trains startling horses passing over the bridge. No such need now as today's horseless carriage crosses the bridge ahead of us. The name however has stuck.

Here we are in Ballasalla awaiting the inbound train from Castletown carrying the singl- line staff we require for passage over the next section of the line. As **No.11 Maitland** approaches the station the fireman is ready to exchange staffs.

Now we are on the final run into Port Erin and the end of the line and the signal giving right of way to enter is clear. All that the footplate crew have to do is ensure they have the flag from the crossing keeper indicating that Droghadfayle road crossing is clear. Trackwork at Port Erin has been altered following extensive track relaying with the IRIS sewage disposal project and now the locomotive can run round its train without occupying the road crossing.

Finally for our footplate trips we join Jeffrey Kelly on **No.15 Caledonia** on a run from Port Erin to Douglas and return. Here we are travelling at speed bunker-first through Colby passing Beatons Lane crossing on the fastest section of the line.

Now our approach is more sedate as we drift into Ballasalla Station and John Elkin stands ready to exchange staffs with Brian Hays, the fireman of **No.15**.

The return trip to Port Erin has started as we approach the White Hoe crossing on the climb out of Douglas towards Kewaigue.

With a good head of steam and full vacuum we are ready to attack the final climb to Ballaquiggin Summit at 230ft after which it is nearly all downhill to Port Erin. The one thing that I found while being privileged to ride on the footplate of several locomotives was how comfortable the ride was on *Caledonia,* particularly when travelling bunker-first.

A view of Colby Station with a double headed train ready to pull away to Port St. Mary and onward to Port Erin.

Here is **No.4 Loch** leaving Crogga Glen running chimney-first to Douglas and climbing the slight grade into Port Soderick Station.

No.4 Loch 'normal way round' drifts into Nunnery Cutting having given two warning whistles as required by the rule book to warn of its approach to Douglas.

Another view of *No.4* this time crossing the embankment over the Santon Burn and approaching Santon Station.

No.11 Maitland starts its final descent into Douglas as it leaves the rock cutting at Keristal and approaches the open cutting at Kewaigue.

No.4 Loch again on the climb out of Douglas approaches Loch Ned, leaving Douglas behind in the background. In summer this area is ablaze with Rosebay Willowherb or to give it its common name "Fireweed" it being the first flower to bloom after the fire of London. It is a common inhabitant of railway trackbeds.

There have been a number of photographs of the Santon embankment and reference to the fact that it crosses the Santon Burn. Well, here to prove the point is the bridge through which the river flows with *No.4* crossing the burn.

Two photographs of civil engineering structures on the line. The first is at Santon where the line crosses the road at Ballavale just before it enters Santon Station. The masonry bridge is quite high and beautifully constructed but more slender than the one carrying the main road to the south over the line at the station.

The second is a recent photograph of the old Kewaigue bridge and the new. The old masonry bridge on the right, viewed from the old road alignment, was narrow and low and for years had been a hazard to commercial traffic particularly as industrial estates developed on the edge of Douglas. The road has now been completely realigned and a new reinforced concrete stone faced-bridge has been constructed to carry the railway.

No.4 Loch again passing through Colby level on the long run in to Port St. Mary from Ballabeg.

No.4 Loch in the cutting alongside Castletown bypass having just passed under Castletown Bridge. In the distance the gates at Mill Road crossing have already been opened to vehicles.

I have included this photograph as a tribute to a good friend and fellow enthusiast. After he retired from politics Peter Craine could not stay away from the railway which had occupied so much of his life and came back as an employee to become the Station Master at Ballasalla. Here he demonstrates the dexterity required to exchange single-line staffs with the incoming train from Port Erin.

No.11 Maitland in the cutting at Keristal. The presence of the works van in the background and the wisps of smoke indicate that sparks from the engines have set fire to the gorse - a problem in dry summers.

No.10 G.H.Wood resplendent in its newly-painted state is a tribute to Beyer Peacock who built it and to those who have cared for it since. The photograph shows its classic lines to advantage. The other photograph shows *No.4 Loch* restored to almost original condition and the coaches are back in the red and cream livery. It is now for someone else to take the pictorial record of the railway into the 21st century.